PIANO · VOCAL · GUITAR

A PENTATONIX *Christmas*

ISBN 978-1-4950-9608-2

HAL•LEONARD®

7777 W. BLUEMOUND RD. P.O. BOX 13819 MILWAUKEE, WI 53213

Visit Hal Leonard Online at
www.halleonard.com

O COME, ALL YE FAITHFUL

Traditional
Arranged by PTX and Ben Bram

Moderately

O come all ye faith - ful, joy - ful and tri -

um - phant. O come ye, O come ___ ye to Beth - le -

hem. ___ O come and be - hold Him, born the King of

5

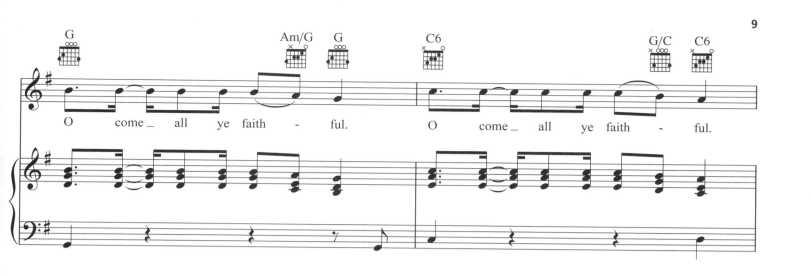

O come _ all ye faith - ful. O come _ all ye faith - ful.

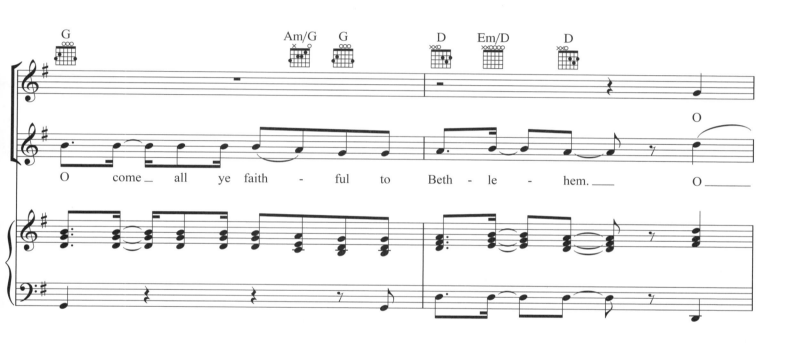

O come _ all ye faith - ful to Beth - le - hem. ___ O _____

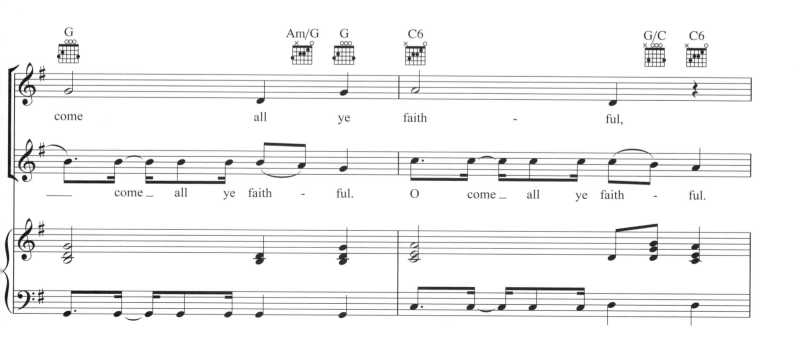

come all ye faith - ful, _____ come _ all ye faith - ful. O come _ all ye faith - ful.

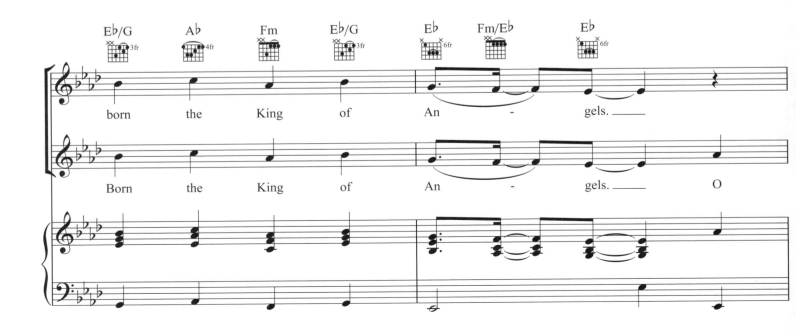

GOD REST YE MERRY GENTLEMEN

Traditional
Arranged by PTX and Ben Bram

Moderately, in 2

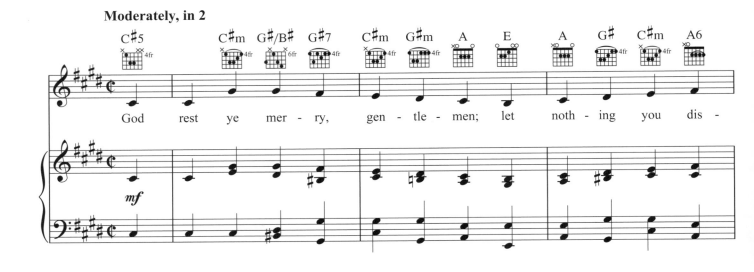

God rest ye mer - ry, gen - tle - men; let noth - ing you dis -

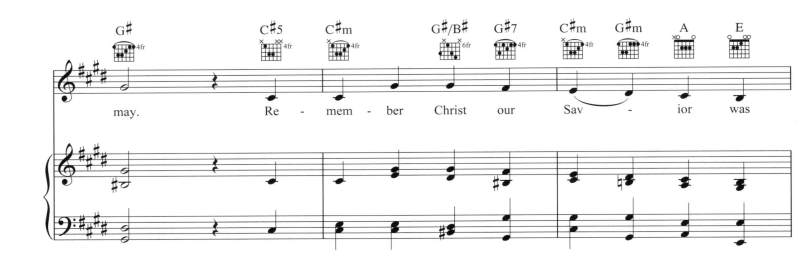

may. Re - mem - ber Christ our Sav - ior was

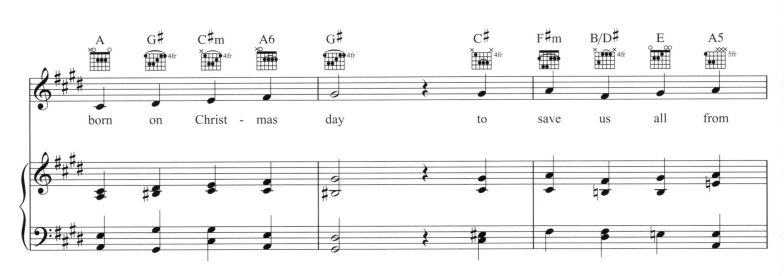

born on Christ - mas day to save us all from

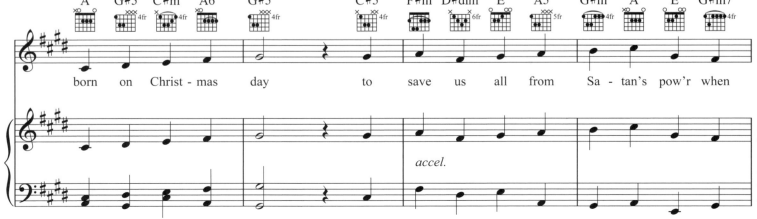

WHITE CHRISTMAS

from the Motion Picture Irving Berlin's HOLIDAY INN

Words and Music by
IRVING BERLIN

UP ON THE HOUSETOP

Traditional
Arranged by PTX and Ben Bram

I'LL BE HOME FOR CHRISTMAS

Words and Music by KIM GANNON
and WALTER KENT

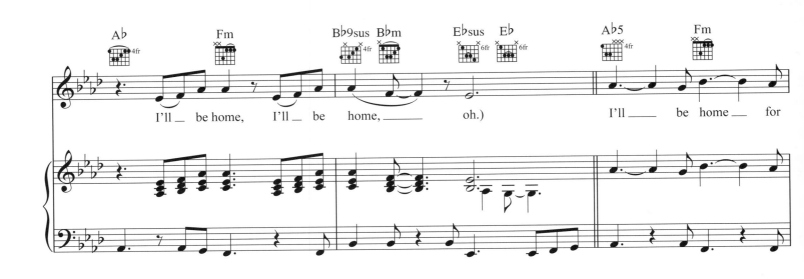

THE CHRISTMAS SING-ALONG

Words and Music by SCOTT HOYING
and KEVIN "K.O." OLUSOLA
Arranged by PTX

GOOD TO BE BAD

Words and Music by SCOTT HOYING
and KIRSTIN MALDONADO
Arranged by PTX and Ben Bram

So bad, __ so bad. __ Good to be so bad, __ so bad. _

__ Good to be so bad, __ so bad. __ Well, it feels so

(good to be bad), (good to be bad), (good to be bad). I've been think-ing 'bout this

COVENTRY CAROL

Traditional
Arranged by PTX and Ben Bram

HALLELUJAH

Words and Music by
LEONARD COHEN

Moderately, in 2

I've heard there was __ a se-cret chord __ that Da-vid played, __ and it

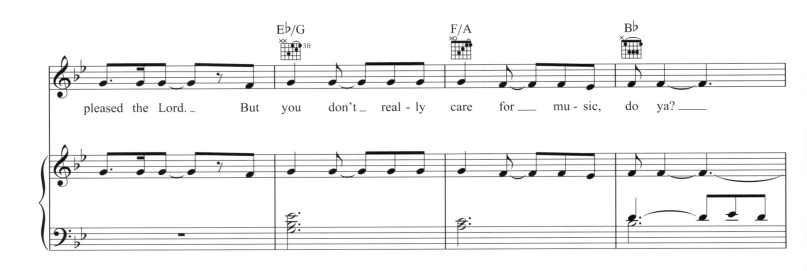

pleased the Lord. __ But you don't __ real-ly care for __ mu-sic, do ya? __

Well it goes like this: the fourth, the fifth, the mi-nor four, __ the

COLDEST WINTER

Words and Music by
ROLAND ORZABAL

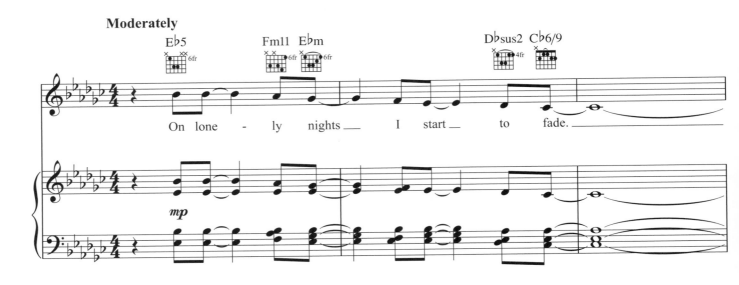

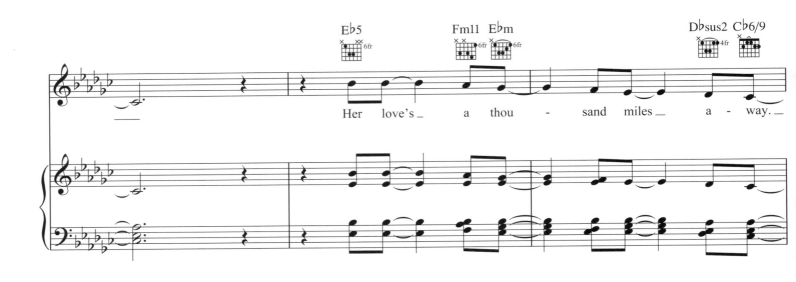

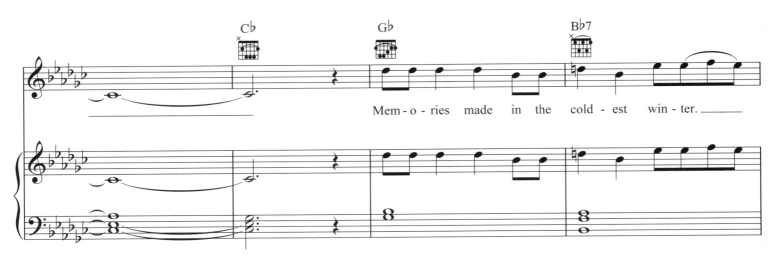

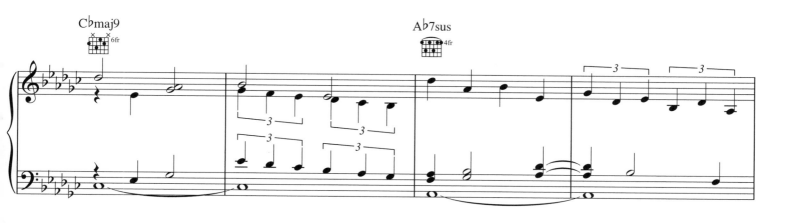

Good-bye, __ my friend. __ Will I ev - er love __ a - gain? __

Moderately fast

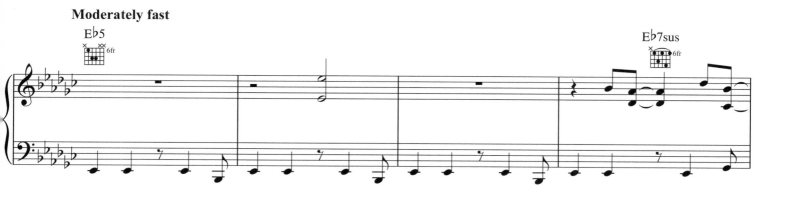

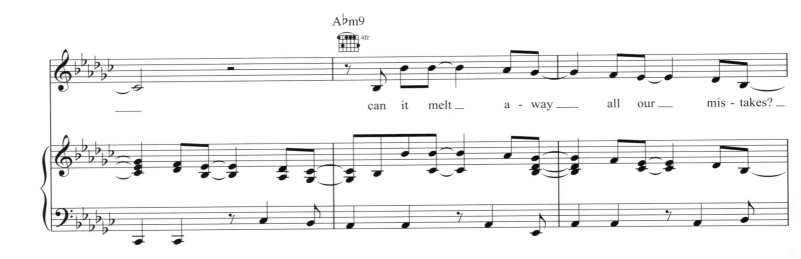

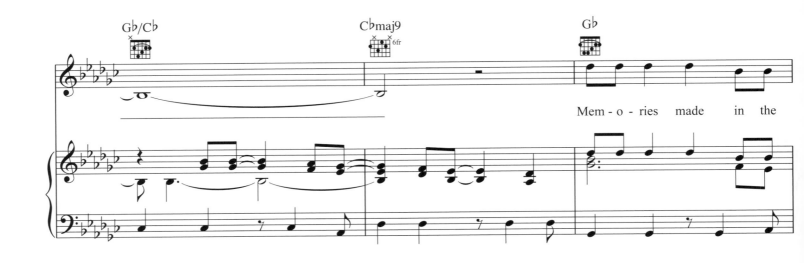

MERRY CHRISTMAS, HAPPY HOLIDAYS

Words and Music by JOSHUA SCOTT CHASEZ,
VINCENT PAUL DIGIORGIO, VEIT U. RENN
and JUSTIN TIMBERLAKE